GROUP

Daniel

LIVING BOLDLY FOR GOD

CWR

Christine Platt

Contents

Introduction

'In spite of present appearances, God is in control.'[1] This is the core message of this intriguing book of Daniel. As such, it is highly relevant for many of us today. When we look around our world, and even our own small corner of it, there are powerful entities – political parties and interest groups – striving for our attention and vying for our support. Sometimes we can feel like insignificant pawns in a mad game. Decisions made 'on high' mean that our income and security can disappear in a moment. Large disparities between rich and poor can mean that justice is hard to find.

Daniel's story reminds us that 'in spite of present appearances, God is in control'. Although the book bears Daniel's name, the subject matter is GOD in giant capital letters! 'The Most High God is sovereign over all kingdoms on earth' (Dan. 5:21).

The book divides neatly into two. Chapters 1–6 are set in the sixth century BC, and its stories are among the most famous in the Bible. Daniel in the lions' den (chapter 6) is a favourite drama opportunity for children. 'The writing on the wall' (chapter 5) has become a phrase well used by many who don't even realise it comes from the Bible.

Chapters 7–12 contain apocalyptic (end times) prophecies, visions and dreams. Even Daniel was stunned and perplexed by what he saw, and even felt 'exhausted' (8:27 – 'sick' in the NRSV), so we should not be too surprised if we also find them difficult to interpret!

There is no dispute that Daniel lived in the sixth century, but these last six chapters have engendered hot debate. Many people argue that no one could foretell the future in such detail and so these chapters must have been written later. Others claim that God, being the God of history, is perfectly able to reveal the future to His faithful servant through dreams and visions, and so Daniel could be the author of the whole book. Jesus Himself attested to his authorship in Matthew 24:15.

Daniel lived during a time when empires were falling and new ones were rising. Nebuchadnezzar, King of Babylon, was in expansion mode and captured Jerusalem in 605 BC. Daniel was carried off into exile with other upper-class young men. The Babylonian Empire, which then ruled the known world, was fabulously wealthy and highly religious. Its people worshipped Marduk (Bel), whose Great Temple towered over the city of Babylon.

The legendary Hanging Gardens of Babylon were said to be an engineering marvel, with water pumped up from reservoirs to irrigate a profusion of flowers, trees and shrubs on tiers of arches. There were luxurious apartments – it was a place devoted to pleasure and excess.

God plucked the teenage Daniel and his friends from the nurture of their homes and families and the worship in His Temple and thrust them into this idolatrous, extravagant culture. King Nebuchadnezzar's plan was that these young men would become enamoured with the ways of Babylon, including worshipping its gods. They would then become useful in its civil service and would also lead their countrymen to acknowledge the superiority of the Babylonian Empire and its way of life.

God had other plans for these young men, however. The future looked bleak, but He was working His purposes out. The prophet Jeremiah records God's words to a beleaguered people in an earlier message that is still true for us today: "'I know the plans I have for you," declares the LORD, "plans to prosper you and not to harm you, plans to give you hope and a future'" (Jer. 29:11). Daniel and his friends needed that reassurance. We can take strong encouragement for our own lives from the way things worked out for them.

Despite the odds stacked against them on the human level, Daniel and his friends showed themselves to be faithful servants of the One True God. King Nebuchadnezzar himself acknowledged that Daniel's God was 'the God of gods and the Lord of kings and a revealer of mysteries' (Dan. 2:47). He made Daniel a top civil servant, and eventually prime minister of Babylon. For 72 years (606–534 BC), Daniel was in the privileged position of being God's witness in the palace, through the reigns of several kings.

In terms of human history, Egypt's dominance had been followed by that of Assyria and now it was Babylon's turn (to be followed later by Persia, Greece and then Rome).

In terms of God's purposes: for a thousand years He had been using the Hebrews to show the idol-worshipping nations who He was, but now His people had been conquered by idolaters. What did this say about the God of Israel? Were Babylon's gods more powerful than Him? God intervened through Daniel and his friends to demonstrate to the world by His miracles who really was the Boss!

Daniel's situation was not conducive to a firm faith and bold witness for God. Our circumstances today are similar. Just as Daniel had to choose whether to conform to the world around him or to obey God, so do we. I pray that in studying this dynamic book we will all be empowered and motivated to make the right choices, so that it may be obvious to everyone around us that we worship the One True and Almighty God!

Notes

[1] Tremper Longman III, *The NIV Application Commentary: Daniel* (Grand Rapids: Zondervan, 1999) p.13.

WEEK 1

Flourishing in a Hostile Culture

Opening Icebreaker

Think about situations where you have experienced a different culture, either overseas or in your own country. How did you feel?

Bible Readings

- 2 Chronicles 36:5–23
- Daniel 1:1–21; 2:1–23
- John 17:13–19

Opening Our Eyes

Nebuchadnezzar thought he was on a roll. His conquest of Judah was going smoothly. He blithely took treasures from Jerusalem – not only sacred objects from the Temple but also promising young men of noble birth. These were the elite of the younger generation, the cream of the crop on whom Judah's current leaders had pinned their hopes for the future. How hopeless they must have felt seeing them being dragged off to Babylon!

Nebuchadnezzar had no idea that, in reality, God had permitted him to do this as a judgment on His people for their disobedience (2 Chron. 36:15–21). Jerusalem fell, the people were scattered and exiled – but in that judgment there was blessing: 'The land enjoyed its sabbath rests' (v.21). Ultimately, God's purified people would return to inhabit the land again and restore His worship under the leadership of Ezra and Nehemiah (2 Chron. 36:22–25).

Daniel and his friends didn't know that the future was indeed going to be bright, but nonetheless they chose to trust God in the abrupt, traumatic changes they faced. They were given Babylonian names to indicate their supposed new allegiance to Babylon and its gods. None of them seems to have protested at that, and yet on the matter of food and drink they chose to take a stand. Why was that? What can we learn from them about how to live in a culture that is hostile to our faith?

Believers today tend to react with 'fight or flight'. Some try to get the culture to change, perhaps by means of petitions, blockades and boycotts. Some even take it to the extremes of violence – for example, bombing abortion clinics. On the other hand, there can be a withdrawal from engagement with the culture – one example being the Amish communities.

Others assimilate into the prevailing culture – maybe afraid to be different, or wanting to fit in.

So, what do we do? 'Daniel endured much cultural assimilation yet he knew where it was appropriate for him to draw the line of distinction.'[1]

It's instructive to note that he made his stand with tact and diplomacy, not with angry gestures and insulting words. Even *in extremis*, with imminent death hanging over him, he made a quiet appeal to the executioner, Arioch (Dan. 2:14). He and his friends poured out their feelings to God, not to the people who were committing the injustice.

What does Jesus say? We are to be in the world, but not of it (John 17:15–16) and 'as shrewd as snakes and as innocent as doves' (Matt. 10:16).

It is futile to expect the pagan or secular worlds to embrace God's standards of behaviour. Jesus' message to them is: Come with a repentant heart and receive forgiveness and grace. He is not saying, 'Change your outward behaviour and all will be well.'

What should our attitude be to those who oppose God's standards? How should we live?

The Dream

God cuts through Nebuchadnezzar's complacency with a terrifying dream. His military successes, his power, his riches, even his gods, cannot give him a peaceful mind. God is setting the next scene. Nebuchadnezzar's wise men are found wanting ... Wisdom from somewhere much higher is needed ... Enter Daniel!

NB – For a fuller discussion of the relationship between faith and culture, see Tremper Longman III, *The NIV Application Commentary: Daniel* (Grand Rapids: Zondervan, 1999) pp.62–69.

Discussion Starters

1. What would Daniel and his friends have felt initially when they were taken away to Babylon?

2. What do you think helped them to continue to trust God?

3. Why did Daniel believe that the royal food and wine would defile him?

4. What can we learn from the way Daniel approached the chief official (Dan. 1:8–14) and Arioch (2:14–16)?

5. How could these thoughts about Daniel help to show a way forward to someone who is asked to do something unethical by their employer?

_____

_____

_____

_____

6. Why didn't the king want to tell his wise men the content of his dream?

_____

_____

_____

_____

7. What qualities did Daniel show in Daniel 2:17–19?

_____

_____

_____

_____

Personal Application

As citizens of a heavenly kingdom, we are all to some extent living in a culture hostile to our faith, whether at work or within our families, as well as in political life and the media. To what extent should we fight it, flee it or assimilate into it? Think about your present situation at work or in your family, or some national issue you're concerned about. How can you be God's person in that place and demonstrate His character of mercy, grace and forgiveness as well as holiness? This calls for divine wisdom – which God has promised to give generously to us (James 1:5). It also calls for courage to be prepared to put your head above the parapet. Are you ready and willing to stand for what is right and do it in a winsome way?

Seeing Jesus in the Scriptures

Jesus, the epitome of holiness, lived in a legalistic religious culture as well as the pagan Roman culture in which the Emperor was a god. He suffered daily criticism and misunderstanding from even His closest friends, as well as severe persecution. Because He was holy, the depth of His pain must have been much greater than ours, but still He empathises with our struggles. What helped Him to face each day with confidence? One thing was that His knowledge and understanding of Scripture enabled Him to answer and silence His critics (Matt. 22:23–33). We have that same Word to help us. Let's follow His example.

Notes

[1] Tremper Longman III, *The NIV Application Commentary: Daniel* (Grand Rapids: Zondervan, 1999) p.66.

WEEK 2

Risking All

Opening Icebreaker

Think about biblical or contemporary examples of believers who bravely stood up for what they believed.

Bible Readings

- Exodus 20:3–6
- Daniel 2:24–49; 3:1–30
- 1 Peter 2:4–8

Opening Our Eyes

Nebuchadnezzar's strange dream really shook him. His wise men with their magic books, on whom he had previously relied, were no help. No wonder he was scared. His anxiety and feeling of vulnerability quickly turned to white-hot anger.

When he was ushered into the king's presence, Daniel briefly sketched out the details of the dream. There has been much debate about what each part of the statue represents. The gold head is the only part positively identified, as Nebuchadnezzar and the Babylonian Empire – recent thinking is that the silver, bronze, iron and clay segments should be viewed more generally rather than as specific empires. It's noteworthy that the materials are of ever decreasing value, while what is stressed is the rock – 'cut out, but not by human hands' – which crushes the statue and then fills the whole earth. This reminds us of the description of Jesus as 'the living Stone' (1 Pet. 2:4–8) which, although rejected by humans, has become the cornerstone of the mightiest – and eternal – kingdom.

Human wisdom tends to believe that humankind goes from strength to strength. God's wisdom says that human empires come and go but God's kingdom endures forever.

Whereas in chapter 1 Daniel used his experience of God and life and his common sense to deal with the king, in chapter 2 he needed and received a direct revelation from God (see 1 Cor. 2:13). Nebuchadnezzar was compelled to acknowledge that Daniel's God is 'the revealer of mysteries'. There is no evidence, though, to suggest that he recognised God as the One True God – as a polytheist he would have happily added Yahweh to his collection of gods.

Conform or Die!

Few of us will ever be confronted with a grotesque statue
and commanded to worship it by an absolute ruler. For
Shadrach, Meshach and Abednego, it was conform or die!

They chose to stand up, literally, for God, knowing that a
horrible death awaited them. They didn't know what God
would do – whether or not He would deliver them. They
did know that many others had already died for their faith,
as people still do today – there is not always a magnificent
deliverance. It is also not clear what their understanding of
heaven was. All they were convinced of was that Almighty
God was the only one worthy of worship. He had made
that clear right from the beginning: 'You shall have no
other gods before me' (Exod. 20:3–6). Jesus reiterated
this when He was asked what the greatest commandment
was: 'Love the Lord your God with all your heart and with
all your soul and with all your mind' (Matt. 22:37). That
leaves no room for any rivals on His throne.

The temptation to worship idols is more subtle in the
postmodern world. Bill Bright of Campus Crusade
challenges us with his question 'Who is on the throne
of your life?'[1] The postmodern answer would be 'myself'.
This becomes apparent in the form of many and various
addictions – to pleasure, comfort, power, relationships,
fame, fortune – some of which seem OK on the surface
and so are more difficult to identify. An honest search of
our hearts before God, however, will reveal our tawdry
motives and misguided thinking. Matthew 6:33 exhorts us
to 'seek first his kingdom and his righteousness', just as
Shadrach and his friends did. Let's take their example to
heart and be courageous in our generation, risking all for
Jesus and His kingdom.

Discussion Starters

1. In what ways did Daniel make sure that God got the credit for the interpretation of the dream?

2. How can we use the symbolism of the rock (Dan. 2:34–35,44–45) to encourage us in difficult times?

3. What motivated the astrologers to denounce Shadrach, Meshach and Abednego? How might such motivation be expressed in today's environment?

4. Read Jesus' instructions to the Twelve in Matthew 10:17–20,24–33. What principles here could stimulate you to be as brave as the people you identified in the Icebreaker?

5. Who might have been the fourth man walking around in the furnace?

_____

_____

_____

_____

6. What did God have to do in order to deliver Shadrach and his friends? What does this reveal about God's power?

_____

_____

_____

_____

7. How can we recognise if the idol of self is on the throne of our own lives?

_____

_____

_____

_____

Personal Application

'Whoever claims to live in [Jesus] must walk as Jesus did' (1 John 2:6). Jesus is our supreme example of how to live with God and not self on the throne. In all our decision-making and our reflection on our attitudes and actions, we would do well to keep uppermost in our minds this question: What would Jesus do?

That will help keep us on track when we're tempted to compromise and let self slink back in and take over. Our culture exerts compelling power – it is not a benign dictator, it is ruthless in its determination to coerce us into its ways. 'But thanks be to God! He gives us the victory through our Lord Jesus Christ' (1 Cor. 15:57). Through Him we can be overcomers.

Seeing Jesus in the Scriptures

Daniel and his friends seem to get top marks in the faith and courage departments. Does that make you feel like a bit of a loser? Let's remember that Jesus' disciples did not always excel. Although Peter exhibited heroic boldness in climbing out of the boat to walk on water, he also failed catastrophically when he denied even knowing Jesus.

Whereas our Saviour gives us an example to follow and His Holy Spirit to empower us, He also understands human weakness. He recognises that most of us have moments of brilliance but also moments of madness when we panic and forget all we know about Him. He is always ready to pick us up again when we turn back to Him in repentance, just as He did with Peter (John 21:15–17).

Notes
[1] Tremper Longman III, *The NIV Application Commentary: Daniel* (Grand Rapids: Zondervan, 1999) p.110.

WEEK 3

First Pride, Then the Crash

Opening Icebreaker

Name some of the world powers and structures that in their day seemed so powerful yet have now – at least to some extent – been overcome.

Bible Readings

- Psalm 73:1–28
- Daniel 4:1–37; 5:1–12
- Philippians 2:3–11

Opening Our Eyes

'First pride, then the crash – the bigger the ego, the harder the fall' (Prov.16:18, *The Message*).

Daniel 4 and 5 tell how two men were foolish enough to be arrogant in the face of Almighty God. As we will see in this session and the next one, God pronounced serious judgment on both of them through His servant Daniel. The difference lies in the response of the two kings to God's word.

You would think King Nebuchadnezzar would have learned his lesson more quickly. He'd seen God stride powerfully into his life in the dream in chapter 2 and in saving Daniel's friends from the furnace in chapter 3. Yet when another dream terrifies him, he still sends for the magicians who'd been so singularly unimpressive in the past!

He seems to have been reluctant to acknowledge that the God Daniel worshipped was the only one who could help him. But perhaps many of us are like that today. Self-help books abound. We sometimes prefer to struggle along in our own independence (which is a form of pride) rather than admit that we need God to help us. Jesus stated it clearly: 'Apart from me you can do nothing' (John 15:5). However much that offends human pride, it's the truth.

Nebuchadnezzar was warned and also given a way out: 'Renounce your sins [and be] kind to the oppressed' (Dan. 4:27). He ignored the warning for a year, and judgment fell on him just as he was enjoying an indulgent moment of self-satisfaction (4:29–30). He went completely mad and lost all his dignity, wealth and power. It took him a long time to 'raise his eyes towards heaven' in repentance. But God's mercy is boundless! Despite all his stubborn arrogance, once Nebuchadnezzar repented, God restored not only his sanity but also his position.

You'd think that his successors, too, would learn from this, but each generation of humankind seems determined to make its own mistakes. Belshazzar compounded his arrogance with blasphemy and idolatry, and even when his knees were knocking in abject fear he didn't remember the astonishing stories about Daniel. Fortunately for him, Queen Nitocris[1] still had her wits about her. 'Get Daniel,' she urged him, 'he'll sort this out!' (5:12).

The encouragement in these stories is that God will deal with arrogant, all-powerful rulers. Many in our world suffer grievously under such oppression, but even though it sometimes seems like the wicked are having it all their own way, Psalm 73 teaches us to look at the bigger picture. We could also apply this principle to those who face overwhelming difficulties in life – perhaps illness, disability, family issues. Such tragedies can seem insurmountable but we can fix our hope on the reality that 'nothing is too hard' for God (Jer. 32:17).

The warning for us is that God will deal with human pride. He has given us clear instructions on how to live: 'He has shown you, O mortal, what is good. And what does the LORD require of you? To act justly and to love mercy and to walk humbly with your God' (Micah 6:8). We are not left to work this out by ourselves. God has given us a living example in Jesus who, even though He was God, humbled Himself, 'made himself nothing by taking the very nature of a servant' (Phil. 2:6–8). Just as kings and leaders should be servants of the people, so we are called to be each other's servants.

Discussion Starters

1. How did pride manifest itself in King Nebuchadnezzar's life?

2. How did it manifest itself in King Belshazzar's life?

3. Why is it so hard for humans, especially those in exalted positions, to humble themselves before God?

4. In what ways do we see pride expressed in the Christian community?

5. In Psalm 73, how does the psalmist view the arrogant? What does he feel about his own life? What is God's perspective on the situation? What enables the psalmist to see God's perspective and how does this change his convictions about God?

---

6. How did Jesus demonstrate humility in His human life on earth?

---

7. What does it mean to 'value others above yourselves' (Phil. 2:3)?

---

8. How can you put Philippians 2:3–4 into practice in your own context – in your family, your church, your neighbourhood?

Personal Application

Do you have a hill or a mountain of difficulty in your life that seems insurmountable? Maybe an illness, a disability, a family or work issue – or maybe something in your own character that you keep working on but can't seem to make progress on? Or maybe there is a world problem that truly burdens you, like child hunger or leprosy?

God doesn't always act as dramatically as He did in these two kings' lives, but these accounts show us that His power is unlimited – and that same power is available to us today.

Determine to pray with faith over whatever concerns you. Find some verses that will lift your mind and heart above these distressing circumstances and on to God, who is full of abundant mercy, extraordinary kindness and supreme power.

Seeing Jesus in the Scriptures

These two kings thought of themselves as above ordinary men and women and above God Himself. By contrast, Jesus, who actually *is* God, put aside His power and authority and compressed Himself into human skin. Imagine, 'He who flung stars into space' limiting Himself to the strength of puny human muscles! He experienced human limitations: he got hungry, thirsty and tired, needed friendship.

He didn't come to earth as a fully-grown adult – He went through all the stages of growth just so He could identify with us. He 'shared ... in [our] humanity so that by his death he might break the power of him who holds the power of death – that is, the devil' (Heb. 2:14). Hallelujah! What a Saviour.

Notes
[1] Tremper Longman III, *The NIV Application Commentary: Daniel* (Grand Rapids: Zondervan, 1999) p.139.

WEEK 4

Extreme Courage in a Crisis

Opening Icebreaker

Think about people whose integrity you value, either in public life or among your circle of friends. How do you recognise integrity?

Bible Readings

- Daniel 5:13–30; 6:1–28
- Matthew 7:1–5
- Luke 9:23–26

Opening Our Eyes

There is a marked contrast between Daniel's attitudes to Nebuchadnezzar and Belshazzar, though both of them were guilty of pride and arrogance. Having observed both men over a period of time, he had been able to assess their characters and qualities. He was truly upset at Nebuchadnezzar's fate, but seemed happy enough to see Belshazzar get his just deserts. God had a redemptive message for Nebuchadnezzar, but His word for Belshazzar was final. There were to be no more second chances (Dan. 5:26–28).

Are we today ever able to say that someone is beyond redemption? Or to tell them: 'Your days are numbered'? Daniel spoke to Belshazzar with a prophet's authority and had an unequivocal message for him. I would suggest that none of us is in that position today. 'Our role is not to judge. Rather it is to offer the good news of repentance and restoration.'[1] (This is not to dismiss the importance of church discipline.) We need to recognise that we, too, have faults and to acknowledge our own blind spots when we are tempted to judge others (Matt. 7:1–5). Wouldn't it be marvellous if the whole Christian community was known for its compassion, humility and love rather than, at times, its judgmentalism and lack of acceptance of others' differences?

The magnificent Babylonian Empire came to a dismal end. The Babylonians were totally unprepared for battle – they were actually having a riotous party when the Persian army overwhelmed them without a fight. It seems that Cyrus, King of Persia, put Darius the Mede in charge of Babylon.

Daniel, though now an old man, was still wise and extremely capable, and he rose to high office. More conflict arose in the court as a result of jealousy, but he emerged with an enviable testimony of integrity. 'They could find no corruption in him, because he was trustworthy and neither corrupt nor negligent' (Dan. 6:4). This incident reminds us of the length some people in politics go to in order to dig up dirt on their opponents. How would we fare if someone delved that deeply into our lives?

When Daniel heard of the edict about praying only to Darius, he responded in keeping with his character. No loud protestations, no petitions, no marches, just quiet obedience to God. We can assume that, in his prayer times, he faced up to the cost of discipleship – his own impending gruesome death.

Jesus' teaching about discipleship, 'Whoever loses his life for me ...', is found in all four Gospels, and in two of them more than once (Matt.10:38–39 and 16:24–25; Mark 8:34–35; Luke 9:23–26, 14:26–27 and 17:33; and, in a slightly different form, John 12:25). 'No other saying of Jesus is given such emphasis.'[2] What does it mean for us to take up our cross daily and follow Him?

Darius realised with horror that he had been tricked by his advisers. He knew that Daniel was a man of integrity and a faithful servant. Twice he exclaimed that Daniel served his God continually. Would people say that about us? Even as the most powerful person in the land, Darius could not change the law. He spent an unhappy night, whereas Daniel had a peaceful time, it seems, while an angel kept the lions' tummies quiet and contented!

Again we see the theme of this book: whatever our present circumstances, God is in control. He was well able to rescue His servant from wicked courtiers and ravenous lions.

Discussion Starters

1. What enabled Daniel to remain humble even though he was given extraordinary abilities and received special revelations from God?

_____

_____

_____

2. How do you think the jealousy of court officials might have affected Daniel?

_____

_____

_____

_____

3. How could Daniel's experience help you when you are criticised?

_____

_____

_____

_____

4. How did Daniel demonstrate that he was a follower of God in his personal life and in his professional life?

_____

_____

_____

_____

5. What did Jesus mean when He said: 'Whoever wants to be my disciple must deny themselves and take up their cross daily and follow me' (Luke 9:23)?

_____

_____

_____

_____

6. What do you think are the factors that help people to face extreme persecution and even death for Jesus' sake?

_____

_____

_____

_____

7. How would you help someone who wanted to grow as a follower of Jesus?

_____

_____

_____

_____

8. What practical things can you do to deepen your personal discipleship with Jesus?

_____

_____

_____

_____

Personal Application

Read

Daniel lived a long, full life. He seems to have taken every opportunity to demonstrate kingdom living in the midst of a demanding secular job surrounded by uncongenial colleagues. His sphere of influence was in the palace and high places of government. Our spheres of influence are no less important, even though they may be smaller and less exalted. Our world is in acute need of seeing living examples of Jesus in all aspects of life – home, work, school, community and church. As you begin each day this week, pray for ideas as to how to demonstrate Jesus to those around you and the courage to do so. 'Shine! Keep open house; be generous with your lives. By opening up to others, you'll prompt people to open up with God, this generous Father in heaven' (Matt. 5:16, *The Message*).

Seeing Jesus in the Scriptures

When we think about radical, costly discipleship, Jesus is our model. When we are rejected, mocked or excluded because of our faith, we know He has been there before us. He can identify and empathise with us and support us in our time of trouble. God, in His wisdom, prompted four writers to tell us the stories of Jesus. (There actually were more than four, but Matthew, Mark, Luke and John have been accepted as worthy of inclusion in our Bible.) If we are serious about being His disciples, we need to immerse ourselves in the Gospels. Reading them in different translations can shed new light on familiar stories, and this will continually refresh and deepen our vision of our sensational Saviour and soon-coming King.

Notes
[1] Tremper Longman III, *The NIV Application Commentary: Daniel* (Grand Rapids: Zondervan, 1999) p.150. For a fuller discussion, read pp.149–151.
[2] *The NIV Study Bible* (London: Hodder & Stoughton, 1987) p.1525.

WEEK 5

Cosmic Battle

Opening Icebreaker

Name some situations in the world today where you yearn for God to intervene. Pray about these.

Bible Readings

- Daniel 7:1–28; 8:1–27
- Mark 13:32–37

Opening Our Eyes

The events of these two chapters took place before those of chapter 5, while Belshazzar was still king in Babylon. These chapters mark a change in the book from stories of historical events to accounts of strange dreams and visions concerning the future and end times. These writings are known as apocalyptic literature.

In his commentary, Tremper Longman III devotes considerable energy to explaining the nature of apocalyptic literature and how to interpret it.[1] A very brief summary is that we should not push the imagery too far and try to make sense of every detail. Also, numbers and timings should be read symbolically and not taken to refer to precise dates and times.

Daniel was 'deeply troubled' and 'appalled' by what was revealed to him, and he struggled to understand. We have the benefit of some history and many scholars' research, but some things remain imponderable. However, these chapters are not in the Bible to confuse us – they are there to add to our conception of God.

In chapter 7, evil powers represented by fearsome mutant beasts terrorise and oppress humankind. Suddenly, the scene changes and the image of God in His judgment hall appears. The last beast is destroyed. The climax is when One 'looking like a son of man' comes to inaugurate His eternal kingdom. This illustrates again the comforting theme of this book. Even though it looks as if evil is having its own way in this world, the reality is that God is in control and He will demonstrate His victory in His time.

Two years later (chapter 8), the angel Gabriel and our knowledge of history help us to make sense of some of the imagery. The ram with two horns is the kings of Media and Persia, and the goat represents Greece.

The 'little horn' (7:8) and the 'fierce-looking king' (8:23) have been identified as Antiochus IV Epiphanes, who attempted to eradicate the Jewish faith and in 167 BC ordered that worship in the Temple should cease. He also murdered many Jews. He was an exceedingly nasty piece of humanity and as such was a forerunner of a worse destroyer who will appear in the last days – the Antichrist. (We will learn more of this individual in chapter 11.) God dealt with Antiochus. He died in 164 BC (8:25).

When we read about people who seem to specialise in evil, we can be tempted to feel somewhat smug and think, 'We would never do things like that.' However, Scripture teaches us that 'there is no one righteous, not even one,' and that 'all have sinned and fall short of the glory of God' (Rom. 3:10,23). Maybe our sins are less visible and seem more respectable than oppression and mass murder, but we are all still in dire need of God's forgiveness. Thank God that we can be 'justified freely by his grace through the redemption that came by Christ Jesus' (Rom. 3:24). The description of this cosmic struggle gives us a glimpse of the real battle raging for people's precious souls. Our forgiveness and redemption have been bought at the highest possible price.

God's message to us in these chapters is one of reassurance that in the midst of so much evil and oppression, He has His own timetable for deliverance. Right from the beginning, we know that He has fought for His people. As Exodus 15:3 puts it: 'The LORD is a warrior; the LORD is his name.'

Discussion Starters

1. What were the characteristics of the 'little horn' (Dan. 7:8,24–25), which has been identified as Antiochus?

2. What do we learn about God from Daniel 7:9–10?

3. What do we learn about Jesus from Daniel 7:13–14?

4. How did Daniel react when confronted with dramatic images of human evil and God's holiness and power (Dan. 7:28; 8:27)?

5. We have the immense benefit of living after the coming of Jesus. What can reassure us when we feel appalled by the horrendous ravages caused by evil world systems?

6. How might you answer someone who claimed not to be a sinner and therefore not to need Christ's forgiveness?

7. How should we respond to the truth that God fights a colossal battle for people's souls (Exod. 15:3)?

8. Read 2 Timothy 4:1–2 and 1 Peter 3:15. What do these verses teach us about sharing our faith?

Personal Application

Jesus is coming back 'in blazing fire with his powerful angels' (2 Thess. 1:7). Fire symbolises judgment, a day of reckoning.

How can you prepare those around you for that day? Befriend them, pray, share your testimony and answers to prayer with them, lend them books, invite them to church or an Alpha course? Imagine the thrill of meeting people in heaven who run up to you shouting, 'I'm here because of you!'

The prospect for those who don't repent is so ghastly that most of us probably prefer not to think about it. They will be 'shut out from the presence of the Lord' (2 Thess.1:9). It is not our responsibility, or within our power, to make them turn to Christ. Our role is to ensure that they understand clearly the choices before them.

Seeing Jesus in the Scriptures

Daniel 7:13–14 is the first reference to Jesus as 'son of man'. He is the only one of the Trinity who knows what it is like to be human. He is fully God and fully man – a unique combination. He can empathise with our humanity and its attendant weaknesses, but He has all the divine resources necessary to help us to live as His people in this world (Heb. 4:15–16).

We are encouraged to approach His throne of grace with confidence and receive His help; but do we sometimes overemphasise His accessibility to us as man and underemphasise our rightful response of worshipping Him as God?

Notes
[1] Tremper Longman III, *The NIV Application Commentary: Daniel* (Grand Rapids: Zondervan, 1999) pp.176–193.

WEEK 6

God Goes to War for His People

Opening Icebreaker

How has God answered your prayers in the past few weeks?

Bible Readings

- Daniel 9:1–27; 10:1–21; 11:1
- Ephesians 6:10–18

Opening Our Eyes

Daniel is now an elderly man, probably in his eighties, but God still has vital work for him to do. As he prayerfully pores over the Scriptures, he understands that the end of the exile is in sight. In Jeremiah 25:1–14, God clearly warned His people that He would judge their sin and, if they did not repent, they would be defeated by the King of Babylon and would be exiled from their land for 70 years. Again, much debate has centred on the calculation of when these years began and ended. The important underlying principle is that God has His timetable and had promised to keep His side of His covenant with Israel and bring them back to their land.

You can almost feel Daniel's heart begin to race as the exhilarating conviction grips him that Israel would again prosper as a nation in her own land. He entreats God on the basis of His covenant promises, not of the people's needs or of their deserving His mercy. Daniel's passionate concern is that God's name should be honoured.

'Lord, listen! Lord, forgive! Lord, hear and act! For your sake, my God, do not delay, because your city and your people bear your Name' (Dan. 9:19).

In keeping with His promise in Isaiah 65:24, while Daniel is still speaking, God hears, and then despatches His answer by the angel Gabriel.

How Daniel must have treasured Gabriel's words 'You are highly esteemed'! Even though he may not have fully understood the explanation, he would have grasped that not only was the exile coming to an end, but one day the Anointed One, the Messiah, would come. The message of this book is repeated: even though things look bad, God is working His purposes out and His triumph is assured.

Daniel is then given an eye-popping glimpse into unseen spiritual realities. You would think he would be used to dreams, visions and miracles, but this is on an unprecedented scale. He needs three angelic strengthenings before he can even get himself together enough to listen. There is truly a mind-blowing dimension to life to which most of us are oblivious.

Yet this startlingly powerful being has been held up by 'the prince of Persia' for three weeks! The latter must also be a strong being, then, who has tried to prevent God's messenger from speaking with Daniel. Gabriel needed back-up from Michael, the 'great prince' who protects God's people (Dan. 12:1), and the battle is ongoing (10:20). Gosh!

What does this episode teach us about spiritual warfare? Longman indicates that there are three battlefields:
• out there in the world – we have ample evidence of demonic evil around us.
• the battle for souls. 'A careful study of the entire Bible indicates that evangelism replaces warfare as we move from the Old to the New Testament.'
• civil war within us as we struggle against our own negative thoughts, emotions and actions.[1]

But we are not alone. God fights for us and has given us spiritual weapons. God's people in the Old Testament fought their battles with swords and violence. New Testament people fight with prayer and faith.

It is interesting to note that Daniel makes no attempt to fight the territorial spirit referred to as 'the prince of Persia' – he leaves that to God and His angels.

Discussion Starters

1. What prompted Daniel to pray (Dan. 9:2)?

2. How did he prepare for his prayer time?

3. Why is humility important when we pray?
   (See 1 Peter 5:5–7.)

4. What aspects of prayer did Daniel demonstrate in
   9:4,5,7a,9a and 16–19?

5. Daniel lived a life of faithfulness to God, so why did he include himself when he confessed the sins of the people (9:5–11)?

_____

_____

_____

_____

6. How can you develop the worship aspect of prayer in your own life?

_____

_____

_____

_____

7. Read Ephesians 6:10–18. Against whom are we fighting (v.12)? In whom should we put our confidence (v.10)? What are our responsibilities?

_____

_____

_____

_____

8. What is the significance of each item of armour?

_____

_____

_____

_____

Personal Application

To have open access to Almighty God through Jesus in prayer is an unbelievable privilege. Even more astounding is that He fully concentrates on each of His billions of children all at the same time. We don't have to rush, queue up or make an appointment. Neither are we a bother to Him. He actually really wants to hear us, whether our prayers be long, short, desperate, angry or worshipful.

Also, part of prayer is listening. It's important to take time to tune in your spirit to that 'gentle whisper' (1 Kings 19:12). Don't let your prayer life become a one-sided business in which you do all the talking. Follow the example of young Samuel: 'Speak, for your servant is listening' (1 Sam. 3:10) – rather than 'Listen, Lord, for your servant is speaking!'

Seeing Jesus in the Scriptures

Our 'enemy the devil prowls around like a roaring lion looking for someone to devour' (1 Pet. 5:8). On the cross, Jesus dealt a death blow to Satan's power and, so to speak, clamped a massive, unbreakable chain around his neck (Col. 2:13–15). That's a helpful picture to keep in mind when you feel under attack. Satan does not have unlimited power; God does! The only reason we are able to live in victory, not defeat, is because of Jesus and His costly battle on the cross.

There will still be skirmishes in the war, but the final outcome is assured victory for God and His people. 'Thanks be to God, who always leads us as captives in Christ's triumphal procession' (2 Cor. 2:14).

Notes
[1] Tremper Longman III, *The NIV Application Commentary: Daniel* (Grand Rapids: Zondervan, 1999) pp.259–262.

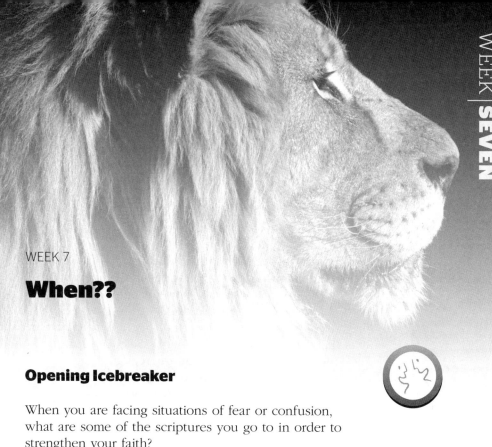

WEEK 7

When??

Opening Icebreaker

When you are facing situations of fear or confusion, what are some of the scriptures you go to in order to strengthen your faith?

Bible Readings

- Daniel 11:2–45; 12:1–13
- Mark 13:1–37

Opening Our Eyes

Some scholars think that Daniel 11 was written at a later date looking back on the events to which it refers. They say that no one can predict that far ahead. However, with God all things are possible. Others believe that it is prophecy and God let Daniel know what would happen in the next few centuries, as well as giving him a glimpse of a much later event: the end of the world as we know it.

Various names have been suggested for the four kings of v.2. The 'mighty king' (v.3) has been identified as Alexander the Great. On his death, his empire was divided between four of his generals – 'the four winds of heaven' (v.4). The kings of the North represent the area of Syria that was eventually ruled by the Seleucid dynasty. The kings of the South represent the region of Egypt, which in time came under the control of the Ptolemies. Judah was sandwiched between these two competing power bases and the third and second centuries BC saw it pass from the sway of one to the other.

The 'contemptible person' (vv.21–35) is Antiochus IV Epiphanes, whom we've already met in Week 5 (Daniel 8). His litany of sins is truly ghastly. He invaded Palestine and went on the rampage against God's people, including desecrating the Temple and abolishing its worship and setting up 'the abomination that causes desolation' – an altar to the pagan god Zeus Olympius. He met his end, 'to be seen no more' (11:19).

Most theologians agree that the king described in vv.36–45 is the Antichrist ('anti' meaning 'against'). He is the epitome of pride and arrogance. He proclaims himself top dog, above every god, and shouts defiance against God Most High. Enter Michael, 'the great prince who protects [God's] people' (12:1). How we need him in this 'time of distress'! In the vision, Michael assures Daniel that, even though everything looks chaotic and desperate, God's people will be delivered. He also gives him an unequivocal promise of eternal life with God (12:3).

What God wants us to realise is that the end will come during a time of massive political and social upheaval, but that He is still on the throne and managing the timetable.

We are then taken back to the river of chapter 10 with the angel hovering over it. 'How long? When?' is the cry – how we would all like to know! Daniel hears the enigmatic answer but he doesn't understand it. He presses for more details, but the angel urges him not to waste time and energy doing mental gymnastics trying to decipher the exact timings, but to get on with his life. 'Go about your business without fretting or worrying. Relax. When it's all over, you will be on your feet to receive your reward' (12:13, *The Message*).

These chapters teach us that judgment definitely awaits those who oppose God, sometimes in this life but most certainly when they meet God in His judgment hall. In addition, a definite reward is promised to those who seek to follow God. How should we respond to this? It should inspire a deep, trustful peace even in the midst of turmoil, knowing that God will sort everything out in the end. Also, a renewed energy to 'lead many to righteousness' (12:3), as well as a determination to 'know [our] God' (11:32) so that we can resist being deceived by the machinations of God-haters.

Discussion Starters

1. What does Jesus teach in Mark 13:1–37 about the signs of the end? (Prophecies can operate on two levels. Some of these 'signs' have clearly already occurred – eg 13:1–2 relates to the destruction of the Temple in AD 70 – but they also prefigure the end of the world.)

2. What instructions does Jesus give in Mark 13?

3. What characterises the people who stay faithful to God (Dan. 11:32,33; 12:3)?

4. Why do you think that neither the angel in Daniel nor Jesus give a clearer indication of the time of the end of the world?

5. When Jesus says 'Be alert ... Be ready ...', how should that affect our daily life and choices?

6. Jesus encourages us in Matthew 5:14 by saying that His people are 'the light of the world'. What is prophesied for God's people in Daniel 12:3?

7. How can you use your answer to Question 6 as an encouragement and stimulus in your own life?

8. Think back over the book of Daniel. What are the main truths you've learned from your study?

Personal Application

These chapters stir us to face the inescapable question: 'What if Jesus came back today? Would I welcome Him with unadulterated joy, or would niggling regrets dampen my spirit?' Another question to ponder is: 'If I knew that my life would end within the next month, what changes would I make in how I use my time, my money and my energy, and how I conduct relationships?'

For most of us, our culture does not encourage us to reflect deeply. Rather, it steers us towards the superficial – things that will make us happy now or meet our needs now. This is a deception to which we need to be alert. Our life in the here-and-now needs to be informed and guided by eternal realities (Col. 3:2).

Seeing Jesus in the Scriptures

One stupendous day, the fabric of heaven will be ripped open and Jesus will make His majestic return – 'in blazing fire with his powerful angels' (2 Thess. 1:7). Fire signifies judgment, and the only way to avoid that searing blaze is to repent humbly and accept the way made open for us. When Jesus was crucified, the curtain in the Temple was ripped 'from top to bottom' – not by human hands – to signify that the way into the Holy of Holies, God's breathtaking presence, is now open (Mark 15:38).

Daniel saw the glimmerings of this good news, and even angels long to look into this mystery (1 Pet. 1:10–12). For us, the message is loud and clear: Jesus declared, 'I am the way and the truth and the life' (John 14:6).

Leader's Notes

Week 1: Flourishing in a Hostile Culture

Aim of the session
1. To explore some of the complexities faced by believers who live in a culture that is hostile to their faith.
2. To understand how to respond to cultural pressures in our own lives.

Opening Icebreaker
This icebreaker is to help people enter into Daniel and his friends' experience, especially as this culture change was forced upon them. They weren't going away for an interesting overseas trip!

Bible Readings
It would be helpful to read all the passages at the beginning of the group session. Getting the members of your group to find the passages and read them will also help any who lack confidence to find their way around the Bible and thereby feel more able to contribute.

Reading the introduction to this study guide gives important background to the book of Daniel. If the members of your group haven't read it, give them a few minutes to do so before starting the discussion. Also, give them time to read the Opening Our Eyes section if they haven't already done so.

Discussion Starters
1. Try to draw out the confusion of Daniel and his friends when they were faced with another language and culture to learn, their homesickness and their concern over what was happening in Judah to their friends and families, their

likely resentment against their captors and their struggle to understand where God was in it all.

2. As friends, they most likely gave each other support and encouragement (Heb. 10:24–25). They may well have known the scriptures that warned of God's judgment on disobedience. They must have acquired good foundations of faith in God at home and in Temple worship, on which they could build in this time of turmoil.

3. The first portion of the royal food and wine was offered to idols. Also, the Babylonians used for food animals considered unclean in Old Testament law and they were not slaughtered or prepared according to Jewish regulations.

4. He didn't make a public fuss, show aggression or complain. He spoke calmly, in private and with wisdom and tact. He negotiated a compromise in Chapter 1 and asked for more time in Chapter 2. He tried not to put the officials in an awkward position with their employer – that is, the King! The situation must have been charged with emotion as mass executions loomed, but he didn't try to mobilise all the exiled young men around his way of thinking and provoke a revolt.

5. It may be that someone in your group could provide a relevant example of this. Or you could discuss the hypothetical case of someone being asked to cut corners on safety or quality control in order to increase output.

6. Possibly he had forgotten it but he knew he had been terrified. Or was it a test, perhaps? The wise men could have given any interpretation of the dream just to save their skins.

7. Faith in God that He would disclose the dream and its meaning to him. He knew he needed his friends' support. He was not a lone wolf but a good team player. His first response was to praise God and honour Him for His mercy in revealing the mystery.

Week 2: Risking All

Aim of the session
1. To be encouraged by God giving wisdom to Daniel and courage to his three friends in the midst of a hostile culture.
2. To help people identify contemporary idols who might be usurping God's place in their lives.

Opening Icebreaker
It is important to acknowledge ordinary men and women who have stood up for their convictions as well as the more well-known ones, such as:
- In the Bible: the woman who anointed Jesus (Mark 14:3–9); Peter saying 'We must obey God rather than human beings!' (Acts 5:19–29); Stephen (Acts 7); Paul on trial (Acts 24–26).
- In recent history: the civil rights activist Rosa Parks; Rachel Scott in the Columbine High School massacre in 1999.

Discussion Starters
1. He stated that God alone could do this (Dan.2: 27–28), and in v.30 he declared: 'I don't have the wisdom for this, but God wanted the King to know what was going to happen.' He referred to 'the God of heaven' (vv.37,44) and 'the great God' (v.45b). Nebuchadnezzar was left in no doubt as to who he was dealing with.

2. Despite attacks against Himself, His kingdom and His people, God will reign supreme and His kingdom will endure for all eternity. Battles may be lost but the war has already been won. God's Church has been through dark times throughout history, but it still endures. In Communist China, the Church was crushed and all the missionaries expelled, but from that time to today the Chinese Church has grown exponentially.

3. They were jealous. Shadrach and his friends were foreigners and yet had been given positions of authority. The astrologers appealed to the King's vanity (Dan. 3:12): 'They pay no attention to *you*, Your Majesty. They neither serve *your* gods nor worship the image of gold *you* have set up.'

'Tall poppy' syndrome – pulling down people who excel. People will find fault where there is no fault. People in positions of leadership unfortunately must brace themselves to receive hostile criticism.

4. We should expect criticism and opposition and not be surprised or shocked by it. 'Forewarned is forearmed.'

The Holy Spirit will give us the words to say when we need them.

People can kill your body but they can't harm your soul. We should be more in awe of God, who holds body and soul in His hands, than of mere human beings.

Believers are greatly loved by God.

If we stand up for God, Jesus will stand up for us before His Father.

5. It might have been an angel, or Jesus (as reflected in His name: Immanuel, 'God with us').

6. He had to encase them somehow in a protective bubble so that the fire, which had already killed the soldiers who threw them in, didn't touch them or their clothing, or leave any scorch marks or smell of burning on them. He had to suspend the laws of nature. He had to make visible an angel or Jesus Himself and enable them all to walk freely around *inside the furnace*!

God's power is absolutely without limit.

7. Prayerfully ask ourselves: Does anything or anyone capture my heart to the detriment of worshipping and serving God? Consider our aims in life, how we spend our time, our money and our energy. Is it all to serve God's kingdom or to build our own kingdom to meet our own needs? Talking this through with trusted friends can help.

Week 3: First Pride, Then the Crash

Aim of the session
1. To show the folly of human pride.
2. To explore ways of serving others with humility.

Opening Icebreaker
Possible responses include: the Roman Empire, slavery, Nazism, the Iron Curtain, the Berlin Wall, apartheid, Pol Pot. The aim of this icebreaker is to encourage members of your group to recognise God's supreme authority over all and in that conviction to pray that He will disempower human structures that oppress people in our world today – eg the drugs trade, human trafficking, prostitution, materialism and greed that favours the rich at the expense of the impoverished.

Discussion Starters

1. Even after God warned him through a terrifying dream, he refused to repent. He insisted that his achievements were down to him alone and did not acknowledge that his power and wealth came from God; he claimed the glory for himself and did not honour God (Dan. 4:29–30).

2. Even though he knew what had happened to King Nebuchadnezzar (5:22), he set himself up against the Lord of heaven. In an attempt to belittle God, he used the sacred vessels captured from the Temple in Jerusalem in his drunken feast and, to cap it all, he praised the gods of the gold and silver and other inert materials of which the vessels were made (5:2–4) – a bizarre act of idolatry!

3. Pride is the oldest sin in the book. Satan was created as a glorious angel but he allowed pride to enter his heart. He wanted to usurp God's place, and he has been playing on humankind's propensity to pride ever since.

The trappings of power and prestige quickly dazzle the brain.

We sometimes think that to serve others is an inferior role.

4. People who are gifted – whether in preaching, healing or music – run the risk of thinking of themselves as better than others, especially if they receive a lot of praise and become famous.

An inverted form of pride is when people feel they have nothing to offer. Basically, they are telling God He didn't do a good job when He created them!

Lack of prayer can indicate an independent, 'I can do it by myself' attitude.

5. The psalmist begins with an unrealistic view of the

wicked – they never have problems and all is well with them – so he envies them.

He feels that his own life is tough, even though he is trying to serve God.

The arrogant think that God is unaware of their sin, but nothing is hidden from His sight.

When the psalmist stops trying to work it out by himself and seeks to understand God's perspective – that is, when he enters the sanctuary – he realises that God will judge the wicked and they will come to no good. When he realises how blessed he is to have God caring for him and giving him security forever, he is then eager to tell others how good God is.

6. Jesus demonstrated humility in His human life on earth by praying often. He lived and associated with ordinary people, not the ruling class. He came to serve (Matt. 20:28) and acknowledged that everything came from God the Father (John 17:7–8).

7. 'Not that everyone else is superior or more talented, but that Christian love sees others as worthy of preferential treatment' *The NIV Study Bible* (London: Hodder & Stoughton, 1987), p.1771.

8. Brainstorm about this. Try to help people to find practical applications they can seek to put into effect over the coming week.

Week 4: Extreme Courage in a Crisis

Aim of the session
1. To explore what is involved in being Jesus' disciples today.

2. To discuss practical ways of following Jesus more deeply in our own lives and situations.

Opening Icebreaker

The aim of this icebreaker is to explore the quality of integrity and how it can be recognised. You could contrast Daniel with the other court officials. You might like to spend a few moments praying for the people you've named and thanking God for them.

Discussion Starters

1. Daniel was constantly aware of his dependence on God and that everything he had came from Him (Dan. 2:20–23). His conception of God was huge and he praised Him often in his prayers. He had vivid examples before him of the folly and peril of allowing pride to enter one's heart.

2. Daniel knew he couldn't trust them as colleagues and would have had to be on his guard. His working life may have been quite lonely because of this. No doubt he prayed to God about it and trusted that God would vindicate him, and therefore he did not see the need to protest publicly.

3. This can be tricky. When we get criticism, we need to ask God and trusted friends whether there is any element of truth in it. If there is, we need to deal with the issue humbly and thank our critic for pointing it out. If there is no truth in it (as was the case with Daniel), we should ask God to vindicate us, forget about it and move on. To defend yourself sometimes makes the situation worse. Again, the advice of trusted friends can help.

4. Daniel demonstrated that he was a follower of God because he:
• prayed regularly, even when threatened with death
• remained humble, even though he was blessed with extraordinary abilities, attained high office and received

special revelations from God
- was consistent - the testimony of Darius was that he was seen to serve God continually
- worked hard, and in fact excelled at his job
- was honest and fair
- accepted the challenge of promotion. He had a realistic assessment of his ability (Rom.12:3) and he didn't suffer from false humility and shrink from the challenge.

5. You might find it useful to look up Luke 9:23 and the verses around it in other versions of the Bible. *The Message* is particularly helpful. Some points to stress are that following Jesus is a day-by-day decision, not a one-off and that doing so will not be comfortable but will involve suffering.

6. People can face persecution and death for the sake of Jesus through the Holy Spirit's presence and strengthening; by remembering that Jesus suffered for them and they follow a suffering yet triumphant Messiah; recalling their previous experience of Him helping them; their knowledge of God's Word and His promises, and through being able to pray at all times and in all places.

7. When you help someone who wants to grow as a follower of Jesus, encourage them to:
- decide to put Jesus first in their lives, and to pray over this regularly
- read the Bible, and especially the Gospels
- pray over what they've read, and keep a note of their thoughts and prayers
- pray for and with others
- take opportunities to share their faith
- belong to a supportive, Christ-centred fellowship in which they can share honestly and learn

8. Encourage people to come up with practical and realistic ideas on how to deepen their personal

discipleship. This could involve their devotional life, some form of service or being alert for opportunities to share their faith in word and deed.

Week 5: Cosmic Battle

Opening Icebreaker

The purpose of this icebreaker is to take our eyes off our own problems so that we can look further afield around the world. Some situations might be child mortality, hunger, poverty, discrimination, war, youth unemployment and people trafficking.

Encourage people to continue to pray about the world issues closest to their hearts and to ask God what contribution they could make towards His solution to these problems. The aim of this is that people will not feel hopeless and helpless in the face of overwhelming evil and need, but rather empowered to seek God's face and work with Him.

Discussion Starters

1. He 'spoke boastfully' and 'considered himself superior'. Again, the sin of pride is highlighted. Antiochus not only spoke but acted arrogantly against God when he resolved to eradicate the Jewish faith and Temple worship.

2. From Daniel 7:9 – 10 we learn:
• from the throne – He is the King
• 'The Ancient of Days' – He is eternal
• from His white clothing – He is holy
• from fire – He is the Judge
• there are many angels (or, possibly, people) with Him – His kingdom is mighty.

3. We can take comfort from the knowledge that Jesus

is the Son of Man with authority, glory and power. He is worshipped by all peoples and His kingdom is eternal.

4. He was deeply troubled in his mind and, physically, in a state of shock; but he kept it to himself and got up and went back to work. (We will see more of Daniel's response in Chapter 9, when he poured out his heart in repentance and praise to God.)

5. We need to maintain in our minds the vision of the risen, victorious Lord Jesus, who has conquered Satan, the origin of evil (Heb. 2:14). We can therefore pray over these situations on the basis of His victory over Satan.

We could also align ourselves with groups that work for justice – as long as they work in a righteous and respectful way.

We also need to remember that God will be sitting on His throne in judgment and nothing and no one will escape His eyes (Heb. 4:13; 9:27).

6. You could remind them of the 'first and greatest commandment': to love God with all their heart and soul and mind (Matt. 22:37–38). They may not have committed murder or adultery, but probably they are not totally committed to God – and James 2:10 teaches that to 'stumble' over just one point of the law is to break all of it.

7. We should recognise how precious people are to God and therefore join in the battle with Him by praying for our friends, our neighbours and members of our families who don't yet know Jesus. We also need to face up to the horrendous danger they are in if they do not repent (2 Thess. 1:8–10).

8. We learn that judgment is coming, and so it is a matter of urgency to share the gospel, 'in season and out of season'.

We shouldn't put it off to a more convenient time. We should be prepared and ready – learn how to answer questions and also to share our testimony in a relevant way. We should be patient, gentle and respectful.

We should also keep the lordship of Jesus uppermost in our minds. Our first priority in life is to please Him, and this may mean sometimes not pleasing other people. This will help us if we are fearful of rejection or mockery from others.

Week 6: God Goes to War for His People

Aim of the session
1. To learn from Daniel's prayer how to deepen our own prayer life.
2. To explore the area of spiritual warfare and learn more about using the spiritual weapons God has given us.

Opening Icebreaker
The aim of this icebreaker is to encourage members of your group to believe that God answers prayer. He answers not only the prayers of spiritual giants like Daniel, for things of national significance, but also our prayers, whether they concern our personal sphere of influence or the wider society. It's important that our prayers are specific – otherwise, we won't know whether or not they are answered.

Discussion Starters
1. He read the Scriptures. We, too, need to use God's Word as a stimulus to prayer. Praying through specific passages for people and situations is powerful and effective. For example, we could pray through the fruits of the Spirit for ourselves and others (Gal. 5:22–23). God will also speak to us through His Word when we ask for His guidance.

2. He fasted to prepare his body and his mind. He put on sackcloth and ashes as a visible sign of humility, repentance and mourning.

3. We need to recognise that God is Lord and knows best. This will stop us being tempted to tell Him what to do! Also, humility helps us to listen and learn from His answers.

4. Daniel demonstrates worship (he keeps a big picture of God in his mind as he prays) and confession of sins. He trusts in God's promises and refers back to God's covenant in the certain hope that He will keep His side of it. He trusts in God's character (9:9a,18b) and petitions God (9:16–19).

5. The people had broken their side of the covenant and there needed to be repentance for them all to come back into relationship with God. Daniel realised that, while his life seemed better than most, he still fell short (Rom. 3:23).

6. We can develop the worship aspect of prayer through singing or listening to worship music or using a psalm of praise. We can use creation as a stimulus, thanking and honouring God for sunsets, flowers, scenery.

Draw out other ideas from members of your group. Some people find candles or a cross helpful.

7. We are fighting against demonic spiritual powers. Often we take aim at human beings – and even our brothers and sisters in Christ – but we need to look further and recognise who the real enemy is.

We should put our confidence in God alone, not our own strength or wisdom. Our responsibilities are to stand firm, trusting God and to use the armour He has given us.

8. The significance of each item of armour is as follows:
- the belt of truth: be honest and sincere, and keep God's Word central
- the breastplate of righteousness: keep close to God and obey Him, recognising that we are righteous only because of Jesus' sacrifice for us, not our own obedience
- feet fitted with the readiness that comes from the gospel of peace – be ready to share the gospel with others
- the shield of faith: resist doubt and focus on who God is and His power
- the helmet of salvation: be sure of our own salvation and our total acceptance by God, and the place reserved for us in heaven
- the sword of the Spirit: keep growing in knowledge and understanding of God's Word
- prayer: essential and indispensable.

Week 7: When??

Aim of the session

1. To grow in understanding about what will happen at the end of the world. God will rescue His people but He has not told us when, and so we should not get sidetracked by human calculations or try to read too much significance into present world events.

2. In the light of coming judgment, to be motivated to use every opportunity to share the gospel in word and deed.

Opening Icebreaker

Some suggestions: Joshua 1:9, Psalm 46:10, Isaiah 41:10–14, Psalm 23, Psalm 27:1 and Psalm 56:3–4.

If members of your group can't think of any verses, you could write some of these out on cards and encourage them to memorise them.

Discussion Starters

If your group is not used to analysing passages of Scripture, you could give them the specific verses noted here to help them to find answers to these questions.

1. In Mark 13:1–37, Jesus teaches about the end times that:
- deceivers will come claiming to be the Messiah (vv.5,21–22)
- there will be wars, earthquakes and famines (vv.7–9)
- there will be persecution of God's people (vv.9–19)
- the gospel will be preached to all nations (v.10)
- God's place of worship will be desecrated (v.14)
- there will be false prophets who perform signs and wonders (v.22)
- there will be dramatic changes in the sky (vv.24–25)
- Jesus will return for His people (vv.26–27)

2. In Mark 13 we are told to watch out that no one deceives us (vv.5,21) and we are told not to be frightened (v.7) and to be on our guard (v.9). Mark 13 also tells us not to worry about how to handle accusations but to trust the Holy Spirit to give us the words to say (v.11). We should be alert and watch for the signs (vv.33,37) because no one knows the exact timing except the Father (v.32).

3. People who stay faithful to God resist being deceived (11:32), they know their God (11:32) and they are wise, and instruct others in the truth, leading many to salvation (11:33; 12:3).

4. The angels don't know when the end of the world will come. Only the Father knows.

Life as a Christian is a life of faith. Jesus gives us enough information for us to live rightly in these days, not in a panic and not in oblivious ignorance. We have been warned and He expects us to be alert and ready to welcome Him back.

5. In our daily lives, we should make every effort to live

in close relationship with Him, learning from Him through His Word and prayer. We should prepare ourselves – not allowing sin to fester in our lives but confessing it and making restitution where appropriate. We should make sure that all our relationships are harmonious. 'If it is possible, as far as it depends on you, live at peace with everyone' (Rom. 12:18). We should also aim to 'let [our] light shine before others' (Matt. 5:16), sharing God's love and truth by word and deed wherever and whenever we can.

6. In heaven, God's people will shine with a dazzling light, like stars forever! Thus, this present life prefigures our life in heaven.

7. God has a high opinion of us and our potential, and this should be a real encouragement for those with low self-esteem. Focusing on being the light of Jesus for those around us will help us to put aside our own fears and inadequacies. We could use this as a daily prayer: 'Lord, guide me in being a light for You today.'

8. It would be helpful to give people some time to crystallise their thoughts – or you might want to schedule an extra session so that the group can fully reflect on these studies. You could ask people to share their biggest encouragement and their biggest challenge.

National Distributors

UK: (and countries not listed below)

CWR, Waverley Abbey House, Waverley Lane, Farnham, Surrey GU9 8EP.
Tel: (01252) 784700 Outside UK (44) 1252 784700 Email: mail@cwr.org.uk

AUSTRALIA: KI Entertainment, Unit 21 317-321 Woodpark Road, Smithfield, New South Wales 2164.
Tel: 1 800 850 777 Fax: 02 9604 3699 Email: sales@kientertainment.com.au

CANADA: David C Cook Distribution Canada, PO Box 98, 55 Woodslee Avenue, Paris, Ontario N3L 3E5.
Tel: 1800 263 2664 Email: sandi.swanson@davidccook.ca

GHANA: Challenge Enterprises of Ghana, PO Box 5723, Accra.
Tel: (021) 222437/223249 Fax: (021) 226227 Email: ceg@africaonline.com.gh

HONG KONG: Cross Communications Ltd, 1/F, 562A Nathan Road, Kowloon.
Tel: 2780 1188 Fax: 2770 6229 Email: cross@crosshk.com

INDIA: Crystal Communications, 10-3-18/4/1, East Marredpalli, Secunderabad – 500026, Andhra
Pradesh. Tel/Fax: (040) 27737145 Email: crystal_edwj@rediffmail.com

KENYA: Keswick Books and Gifts Ltd, PO Box 10242-00400, Nairobi. Tel: (020) 2226047/312639
Email: sales.keswick@africaonline.co.ke

MALAYSIA: Canaanland Distributors Sdn Bhd, No. 25 Jalan PJU 1A/41B, NZX Commercial Centre,
Ara Jaya, 47301 Petaling Jaya, Selangor. Tel: (03) 7885 0540/1/2 Fax: (03) 7885 0545
Email: info@canaanland.com.my

Salvation Publishing & Distribution Sdn Bhd, 23 Jalan SS 2/64, 47300 Petaling Jaya, Selangor.
Tel: (03) 78766411/78766797 Fax: (03) 78757066/78756360 Email: info@salvationbookcentre.com

NEW ZEALAND: KI Entertainment, Unit 21 317-321 Woodpark Road, Smithfield, New South Wales
2164, Australia. Tel: 0 800 850 777 Fax: +612 9604 3699 Email: sales@kientertainment.com.au

NIGERIA: FBFM, Helen Baugh House, 96 St Finbarr's College Road, Akoka, Lagos.
Tel: (01) 7747429/4700218/825775/827264 Email: fbfm_1@yahoo.com

PHILIPPINES: OMF Literature Inc, 776 Boni Avenue, Mandaluyong City. Tel: (02) 531 2183
Fax: (02) 531 1960 Email: gloadlaon@omflit.com

SINGAPORE: Alby Commercial Enterprises Pte Ltd, 95 Kallang Avenue #04-00, AIS Industrial
Building, 339420. Tel: (65) 629 27238 Fax: (65) 629 27235 Email: marketing@alby.com.sg

SRI LANKA: Christombu Publications (Pvt) Ltd, Bartleet House, 65 Braybrooke Place, Colombo 2.
Tel: (9411) 2421073/2447665 Email: christombupublications@gmail.com

USA: David C Cook Distribution Canada, PO Box 98, 55 Woodslee Avenue, Paris, Ontario N3L 3E5,
Canada. Tel: 1800 263 2664 Email: sandi.swanson@davidccook.ca

CWR is a Registered Charity – Number 294387
CWR is a Limited Company registered in England – Registration Number 1990308

Courses and seminars

Publishing and new media

Conference facilities

Transforming lives

CWR's vision is to enable people to experience personal transformation through applying God's Word to their lives and relationships.

Our Bible-based training and resources help people around the world to:

- Grow in their walk with God
- Understand and apply Scripture to their lives
- Resource themselves and their church
- Develop pastoral care and counselling skills
- Train for leadership
- Strengthen relationships, marriage and family life and much more.

Our insightful writers provide daily Bible-reading notes and other resources for all ages, and our experienced course designers and presenters have gained an international reputation for excellence and effectiveness.

CWR's Training and Conference Centres in Surrey and East Sussex, England, provide excellent facilities in idyllic settings – ideal for both learning and spiritual refreshment.

CWR Applying God's Word
to everyday life and relationships

CWR, Waverley Abbey House,
Waverley Lane, Farnham,
Surrey GU9 8EP, UK

Telephone: **+44 (0)1252 784700**
Email: **info@cwr.org.uk**
Website: **www.cwr.org.uk**

Registered Charity No 294387
Company Registration No 1990308

Dramatic new resource

Bible Genres
– Hearing what the Bible really says
by Andy Peck

Explore seven of the major genres used by writers of the Bible and consider how each style reflects more deeply what God is saying in His Word.

72-page booklet, 210x148mm
ISBN: 978-1-85345-987-0

The bestselling *Cover to Cover* Bible Study Series

1 Corinthians
Growing a Spirit-filled church
ISBN: 978-1-85345-374-8

2 Corinthians
Restoring harmony
ISBN: 978-1-85345-551-3

1 Timothy
Healthy churches –
effective Christians
ISBN: 978-1-85345-291-8

23rd Psalm
The Lord is my shepherd
ISBN: 978-1-85345-449-3

2 Timothy and Titus
Vital Christianity
ISBN: 978-1-85345-338-0

Acts 1–12
Church on the move
ISBN: 978-1-85345-574-2

Acts 13–28
To the ends of the earth
ISBN: 978-1-85345-592-6

Barnabas
Son of encouragement
ISBN: 978-1-85345-911-5

Bible Genres
Hearing what the Bible really says
ISBN: 978-1-85345-987-0

Daniel
Living boldly for God
ISBN: 978-1-85345-986-3

Ecclesiastes
Hard questions and
spiritual answers
ISBN: 978-1-85345-371-7

Elijah
A man and his God
ISBN: 978-1-85345-575-9

Ephesians
Claiming your inheritance
ISBN: 978-1-85345-229-1

Esther
For such a time as this
ISBN: 978-1-85345-511-7

Fruit of the Spirit
Growing more like Jesus
ISBN: 978-1-85345-375-5

Galatians
Freedom in Christ
ISBN: 978-1-85345-648-0

Genesis 1–11
Foundations of reality
ISBN: 978-1-85345-404-2

God's Rescue Plan
Finding God's fingerprints
on human history
ISBN: 978-1-85345-294-9

Great Prayers of the Bible
Applying them to our lives today
ISBN: 978-1-85345-253-6

Hebrews
Jesus – simply the best
ISBN: 978-1-85345-337-3

Hosea
The love that never fails
ISBN: 978-1-85345-290-1

For current prices or to order visit www.cwr.org.uk/store
Available online or from Christian bookshops.

Cover to Cover Every Day
Gain deeper knowledge of the Bible

Each issue of these bimonthly daily Bible-reading notes gives you insightful commentary on a book of the Old and New Testaments with reflections on a psalm each weekend by Philip Greenslade.

Enjoy contributions from two well-known authors every two months and over a five-year period you will be taken through the entire Bible.

Only £2.95 each (plus p&p)
£15.95 for UK annual subscription (bimonthly, p&p included)
£14.25 for annual email subscription
(available from www.cwr.org.uk/store)

 **Individual issues available in epub/Kindle formats**

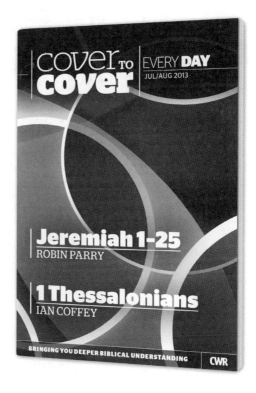

Cover to Cover Complete – NIV Edition
Read through the Bible chronologically

Take an exciting, year-long journey through the Bible, following events as they happened.

- See God's strategic plan of redemption unfold across the centuries
- Increase your confidence in the Bible as God's inspired message
- Come to know your heavenly Father in a deeper way.

The full text of the NIV provides an exhilarating reading experience and is augmented by our beautiful:

- Illustrations
- Maps
- Charts
- Diagrams
- Timeline

Key Scripture verses and devotional thoughts make each day's reading more meaningful.

ISBN: 978-1-85345-804-0